SELF CA[RE]
FOOD

SELF CARE ZINE: FOOD

Curated by Rachelle Abellar
Cover art by Christopher Duran
Edited by Sarah E. Hoffman
With Special Thanks to Adrienne Fox

TABLE OF CONTENTS

Eat What You Want, When You Want 4
Farmers and Foodies 6
Kitchen Essentials 7
Time for Nachos 9
Inventory 10
Microwave Mug Cupcake 11
Best Foods For When You're Under the Weather 12
Nutella 13
The Chemistry of Buttermilk Pancakes 14
Vegetarian Chili 16
How To: Efficiently Seed a Pomegranate 19
London Fog 20
Café (Tacit Knowledge) 24
Food That Can Help Boost Your Mood 25
Eat to Live 27
The Covenant of the Wing 28
How To: Pit an Avocado 30
Chocolate Avocado Pudding 31
Summer Sangria 32
Connect the Dots 34
Eating While On Your Period 35
Vegan Cookie Recipes 36
One Pot Spaghetti Alla Puttanesca 38
Baking 40
Homemade Dinner Rolls 42
Best Popcorn 43
Stevie's Grammie's Peanut Butter Cookies 44
Food Staples for Cooks on a Budget 48
Comfort Foods 50
Chunky Tomato Soup 51
Reaching for New Recipes 52
Food Resources 54
Zine Contributors 55

EAT WHAT YOU WANT, WHEN YOU WANT

By Rachelle Abellar

TW: dieting, weight loss, eating disorders

In our a diet-centric culture, it's easy to internalize toxic ideas about weight and assign moral value to food. We're taught what we should and shouldn't eat, and when to eat it. Our media is plagued with headlines like, "24 Foods You Should Avoid at All Costs," "10 Diet Foods that Actually Make You Fat," and my personal favorite "The Baby Diet: How Eating Like a Toddler Could Help You Lose Weight." We associate the feeling of guilt with food. We label salads as a "clean" food and pizza as "dirty" or off limits. We set designated free days or cheat meals. We describe good foods as real food and bad foods as sinful. You get the idea.

The truth is, **food is neither good or bad**. It is merely energy your body needs to function and survive. When we assign moral value to food, we also end up assigning moral value to ourselves for eating it. This is a dangerous way of thinking that can lead to disordered eating habits, extreme dieting, and physiological changes that can negatively affect both your physical and mental health.

I am fat. I've always had a complicated relationship with food. Five years ago, I made the decision to start making peace with my body and mending my relationship with food. When I first started getting into fat acceptance, I came across the Health at Every Size (HAES) movement and it was life-changing. According to the HAES website, the movement is "based on the simple premise that the best way to improve health is to honor your body. It supports people in adopting health habits for the sake of health and well-being (rather than weight control)." It was through HAES that I discovered the concept of intuitive eating.

When we subscribe to strict diets, we are basically saying we don't trust ourselves to make good decisions. Honoring your body includes trusting your body to make nourishing food choices. Intuitive eating is a hunger-based approach to eating: Listen to your body and eat when you're hungry. Stop when you're full. It takes the focus away from the dietary aspects of nutrition so we are not limited to eating good foods and avoiding bad foods. In the book *On Eating*, author Susie Orbach lists the five keys to intuitive eating:

1. Eat when you are hungry
2. Eat the food your body is hungry for
3. Find out why you eat when you aren't hungry
4. Taste every mouthful
5. Stop eating the moment you are full

The concept may sound like it should be common sense, but when you have a history of dieting or following socially imposed rules about eating, it can be quite difficult. I have spent so much of my life dieting and consumed with restricting calories that I struggled with recognizing my body's internal hunger/satiety cues. To remedy this, I've dedicated a huge part of my own self care to the practice of intuitive eating.

Over time, I was eventually able to stop viewing food as the enemy and start viewing it as something enjoyable, nourishing, and satisfying (on so many levels). I no longer feel consumed by counting calories or obsessing about gaining weight. I am able to enjoy eating without guilt. I've noticed that a lot of times when I think I really want something, I actually don't want it at all. And I feel healthier, happier, more present, and more energetic.

This is merely an account of my experience with intuitive eating. Please note that I am not a medical doctor. I encourage you to do some research (there is so much information out there!) and/or consult a qualified health care professional before making major changes to your diet. Good luck!

FARMERS AND FOODIES

By Sarah E. Hoffman

Food is often vilified (by society and by ourselves), but food can be a wonderful tool for community, social change, personal development, and, of course, self-care. The vilification (and resulting problems) of food in modern society are entrenched as many of the social exchanges that occur over food are fundamentally flawed. Fast food meals, pre-packaged food, and bottomless pop when combined with weight loss regimes, impossibility skinny women in media, and the righteousness of health food make it darn near impossible to have a healthy relationship to food. The solution to the vilification of food in our society is two-pronged requiring the involvement of farmers and foodies.

Farmers once made farming decisions based on social, environmental, and/or personal concerns and motivations. The industrialization of the farming process has eradicated and replaced this multifaceted decision making process with one that only considers the needs of industry. Examples include replacing diversity with monocultures and taste with ease of shipping. To resolve the problems of corporate control over our food supply the small farmer has to take responsibility for their part in the loss of agricultural knowledge and importance in society. The farmer has to emerge as an expert in food production, land management, and animal husbandry. **Farmers have to become, once again, responsible for food.** It's up to the ingenuity, creativity, and long-term agricultural knowledge of true food warriors – farmers – to reinvent, recreate, and re-imagine our dysfunctional agricultural relationship into one that respects the land, the workers, and the food. The solution to the problems of industrial agricultural do not lie in the past – in an idealized version of small family farming – rather they lie in the future. In re-imagining our relationship and interactions with and over food. An agricultural relationship that savors an enlightened, respectful, and honest relationship with food will give us the motivation, insight, and knowledge to recreate our relationship with the land.

The role of foodies? Why that's up to you! As foodies, we have to disengage from corporate control over our food and our interactions with

FOOD TIP: It's important to stick to regular eating schedules when sick because consuming fewer calories than normal can restrict the body's ability to heal.

food. We have to make active decisions about our ideal relationship with and over food and make changes to reflect that opinion. Refuse to shame and be shamed regarding your relationship to food. Enjoy

KITCHEN ESSENTIALS
By Jon Conley

CHEF'S KNIFE (http://goo.gl/WCwKi): A Chef's Knife is the lynchpin of all chopping and cutting work; never cut with a dull knife; learn the basic knife skills before you start. The Fibrox 8-Inch Chef's Knife is the best value. Here's a great training video: http://youtu.be/yGsoUmQjio8.

CUTTING BOARD (http://goo.gl/L0VH1W): OXO brands are ergonomic, non-slip cooking tools of reputable quality. You can find them at any kitchen supply store or section (at Target, for example).

PEELER (http://goo.gl/ZZFL1x): OXO Pro Swivel Peeler comes out on top for me. This tool will be invaluable to you, when it comes to peeling fruits and vegetables. It will pay for itself in the amount of time in saves you in about a week.

A DECENT PAN (http://goo.gl/jrhiKj): Cast Iron skillets are great. The 10" one is big enough to cook two servings. You will cook the best meals of your life using them. Cast iron is unique, in that they are 'non-stick' by virtue of caked-on layers of carbonized oil (safer than teflon coatings); so you don't use soap to clean them – just scrub them out with a dish scrubber and hot water (no machine washing). Watch this to learn more: http://youtu.be/Y7jW0r5ZcHc.

A BOX OF KOSHER SALT (http://goo.gl/14j9YF): Kosher salt is thick (think about the kind of salt you eat on a soft pretzel), and it goes a long way (this box should last you months). The flavor is incredible, and you use less salt than you would if you cooked with table salt.

QUALITY COOKING OIL: Go to Costco for Olive Oil, if you can. Trader Joe's is affordable, and their sunflower seed oil is great (and great for most cooking). Remember: different oils have different "smoke points." You typically never need more than a few teaspoons of oil while cooking. Read about grease fire safety before getting started: http://www.thekitchn.com/kitchen-safety-how-to-put-out-138233.

A QUALITY OVEN MITT OR TOWELS (http://goo.gl/6RN4e5): Always double-wrap a (dry) towel around your pan handles, or invest in a quality silicon oven mitt to avoid serious burns.

A METAL SPATULA (http://goo.gl/o7zHfa): Try not to dig into your pan with your spatula, as you will damage the pan. That said, I frown upon plastics being used around high heat. Get yourself a quality spatula to cook with (and some wooden utensils).

A FIRE EXTINGUISHER (http://goo.gl/M7KGzP): Hopefully, you never need this. In the event of a kitchen fire (or any fire), it's good to have. Never use water on a grease fire. It's worth the ~$20 to be safe.

"Just remember this: the same way that food isn't love, it's not hate, either. It's not the enemy. Food is a gift you give your body; it keeps you alive and can even, if it's really good, offer a wildly intense sensual pleasure. Stop, close your eyes, really listen to your body. What does it want to eat right now, what will make it feel wonderful? Go eat that thing."

Betsy Cornwell, "7 Gifts To Give Yourself Right Now"

FOOD TIP: When cooking, fatigue can be an issue, so take frequent breaks and keep a chair or stool nearby in case you need to sit down.

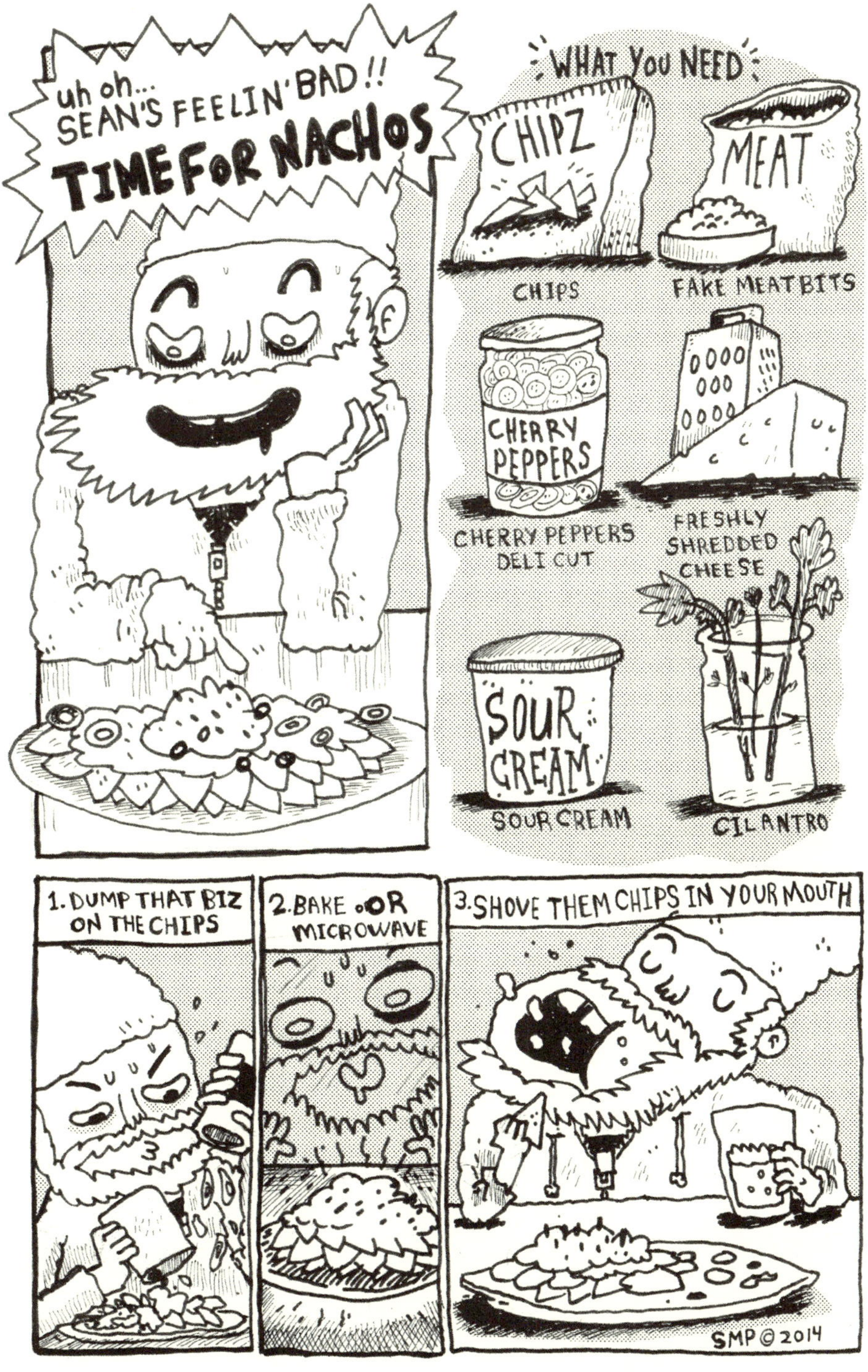

BY SEAN POPPE

INVENTORY

- Holy Grail Sundae
- Flaming Mallow Sword
- Hot Cauldron of Oxtail Stew
- Burrito Supreme Being
- Bucket O' Banana Puddin'
- Everlasting PB Cookies +5
- Basil Lemonade Elixir
- Cheese Jam War Hammer
- The Whole Dozen

EQUIPPED

- Hot Dog Classic
- Macaroni Pizza Shield
- Buttered Banana Bread

BY DANIELLE MARTIN

MICROWAVE MUG CUPCAKE
By Jade Gordon

I tried a few different recipes for Microwave Mug Cupcakes, and this was what I came up with. If you portion out the dry ingredients into small bags or containers, you can just add the wet ingredients when you want to make one!

Fun things to drop in:
Peanut butter, crushed up hollow Easter bunny chocolate, toasted coconut... It is also excellent topped with raspberry jam or syrup, whipped cream...

Ingredients:
2 tbps flour
2 tsp cocoa powder (preferable dark chocolate formulations, Valrhona if you can!)
3 tsp sugar (adjust to taste)
1/4 tsp baking powder
1 pinch salt
1 tbps oil (canola, peanut, or appropriately flavored oil)
2 vvv milk

Directions:
Mix all the dry ingredients, then add the wet and stir well. Microwave for slightly more than 1 minute, my microwave took about 1 min. and 8 seconds. Less and it will have a little bit of a molten middle, but it tastes better fully cooked.

FOOD TIP: If you over-salt a pot of soup, drop in a peeled potato to absorb some of the excess salt.

TRY THIS!

If you aren't sure how fresh your eggs are, place them in a bowl of water. Eggs that stay on the bottom of the bowl are fresh and floaters have gone bad. If only one end tips up, it is less fresh and should be consumed soon.

BEST FOODS TO EAT WHEN YOU'RE UNDER THE WEATHER

NAUSEA: ginger ale, ginger tea, bananas
CONGESTION: hot tea, broth-based soups
COUGHING: cherries, oranges
SORE THROAT: honey, honey mixed into hot tea, pure juice popsicles
DEHYDRATION: water, tea, pure juice popsicles, cold-pressed green juice
EASILY DIGESTABLE PROTEINS: eggs, tofu, chicken, yogurt

"Food comes with a lot of weird baggage, especially for girls, and we need drop that baggage off at the front desk real quick. There are so many trendy (and often extreme) diets that the only one that is going to work for you is eating what you want. We all know that too little of anything isn't good for us and too much of anything isn't good for us either. Enjoy what you eat and don't be ashamed by it."

Martina Dorff, "Sad Girls Guide to: Fat Acceptance"

BY ANTONIA TSANGARIS

THE CHEMISTRY OF BUTTERMILK PANCAKES

By Erica McGillivray

The women in my family aren't known for culinary delights or secret family recipes. People don't rush to our dinner tables. Flat palettes from the Midwest, coming to America from famines in Ireland stick close to canned beans, boiled potatoes, and meat.

There have been one or two exceptions over the years. My maternal grandmother Marlene's pecan pies and nut pudding, and my paternal great-grandmother Peggy's buttermilk pancakes. I don't recall my great-grandmother ever making them for me herself, but my grandmother Evelyn did. She cooked them in her log cabin home, on an antique wood burning stove, using great-grandma's cast iron pancake griddles. My grandmother made them for the guests of her bed and breakfast. But most importantly, she made them for us, her grandchildren.

Her pancakes were fluffy and tasted like pure heaven. I loved them with jam or peanut butter. My brothers drowned them in maple syrup. Sometimes grandma would pull out her homemade blackberry syrup. But the pancakes were even good just with butter, hot off the stove. I'd gobble them down sitting at the long pine wood table with its matching benches. My cousins and I learned patience and how to take turns as grandma cooked pancakes two by two.

Cooking is chemistry. Between the crackling wood and the cast iron, there was something special about those pancakes. Something that made me rise out of bed at any hour just to eat them, and I have never been a morning person.

When not cooked on that stove and on those griddles, some of the pancakes' magic, some of their chemistry got lost. They were still delicious enough for me to turn my nose up at Krusty's or iHop. But the pancakes weren't the same. They're never quite the same as I remembered.

FOOD TIP: If you need to measure syrup or honey, swish vegetable oil around in the measuring cup first to prevent sticking.

My family, we tried our best to fill in the gaps. My father would make shapes: cacti and snowmen. My brothers and I made patterns with chocolate chips. My mom would add blueberries and keep making them even after my parents divorced. And we'd add moments too. Pancakes were what I asked for after being in Europe for three weeks as a teenager and missing the comforts of home. I had them for dinner on my 18th birthday. I make them on snow days. Or bright sunny days.

My grandmother sold the log cabin years ago, and she passed away last Christmas. I don't know what happened to those pancake griddles. But buttermilk pancakes have become a ritual. One that says "welcome home" or "let's hang out in our flannel pjs today." One that says, today's going to be good, now have a pancake or maybe four. Enjoy.

MOTHER'S BUTTERMILK PANCAKES
Makes 4 servings

Ingredients:
2 eggs
1/4 cup vegetable oil
2 3/4 cups buttermilk
2 cups flour
1 1/4 tsp baking soda
3/4 tsp baking powder
1/4 tsp salt

Directions:
1. Beat eggs with a wire whisk.
2. Beat the oil and buttermilk into the eggs until well-blended.
3. Sift together flour, soda, baking powder, and salt.
4. Stir dry ingredients into the egg mixture, stirring only enough to moisten. (Adjust flour as needed.)
5. Pour pancakes onto a hot, greased griddle, turning when bubbles appear.
6. Serve with jam, berry syrups, maple syrup, or honey.

FOOD TIP: Tap an egg firmly on a flat surface rather than against a bowl edge so that it cracks more cleanly and you don't drive little shell pieces inside.

vegetarian chili

ingredients

- 3 cans of beans* rinsed and drained
- 1 can of diced tomatoes
- 2 tbsp of vegetable oil
- 1 medium yellow onion, chopped finely
- 1 oz unsweetened/dark chocolate
- 3 tbsp chili powder
- 2 tsp cumin
- 2 tsp paprika
- 2 bell peppers, chopped roughly
- 2/3 garlic cloves chopped finely
- 1 tsp of chipotle chili paste/canned chipotle chilis
- a tall glass of chocolate stout
- 1½ cups of frozen sweetcorn
- 2 tsp of table salt
- cracked black pepper, to taste

* I generally use kidney beans and cannelini beans. Feel free to substitute your favourite kind of beans!

BY DALE O'FLAHERTY

sauté the chopped onion for five mins on medium heat

pulse the chopped tomatoes until smooth like salsa

set aside

add the chopped garlic and spices. cook for about 30 seconds

FOOD TIP: Freeze cranberries before you grind or chop them to avoid a huge mess.

add the pulsed tomatoes and the rest of the ingredients*

*except the sweetcorn

cook on medium heat for 15 mins

stir in the frozen corn and cook for 2 mins. Season with salt and pepper and serve with rice (optional).

—I'm really proud of this recipe! It's rich, hearty, it keeps really well, it makes a ton of leftovers. It feels really good to prepare for days when I don't have the energy to cook properly. It can also be made vegan! Just substitute vegan dark chocolate.

Enjoy!   —dale o'flaherty

PHOTO BY ANITA SARKEESIAN

HOW TO:
EFFICIENTLY SEED A POMEGRANATE

By Adrienne Fox

1. Using a sharp knife, cut the fruit in quarters.
2. Place a mixing bowl in the sink and grab an apron (there will be some splatter).
3. Hold one quarter in your hand with skin-side up. Take a wooden spoon and whack the skin to release seeds into your hand. Let the seeds fall into the bowl.
4. Repeat process with each quarter.
5. To remove any remaining seeds stuck inside, break the quarters open and either use the method above or remove with your fingers.

FOOD TIP: Before cooking brussels sprouts, slit them halfway through the base. They'll cook evenly and quickly.

London Fog

kgros

I live in Vancouver, where winters are as grey & rainy as they come.

Fancy tea lattes are my go-to pick me up, but they're expensive & I'm not always up for leaving the house.

BY KATHLEEN GROS

So here's how I make London Fogs at home:

earl grey tea, sugar, milk, vanilla

- fill your mug about 1/3 of the way with boiling water & steep your tea bag

- add your desired sweetner — I like 2 spoonfuls of sugar

FOOD TIP: Quick breads, such as banana bread, will cut in neater, thinner slices a day after baking.

- heat the milk, add a splash of vanilla & whisk vigorously & constantly

you'll see bubbles starting to form—keep whisking until you have the desired amount of foam.

"never enough foam!"

FOOD TIP: *When you sit down to eat a meal, take 3 breaths before eating. Slow down, calm, and center yourself. It helps digestion and makes your meal more nourishing on every level.*

○ *carefully pour your hot, frothy milk into your mug & enjoy!*

♡ kagly

FOOD TIP: *Soak bitter greens, like arugula or kale, in a bowl of ice water in the fridge for about an hour to cut their bitterness.*

CAFÉ (TACIT KNOWLEDGE)
By Adam Johnson

A little café in a little town in the pleasant ruin that is Portugal. My friend and I, half awake, walk the quiet alley ways and half-streets in the distant winter sun. Two Americans, speakers of Spanish and Italian, but not Portuguese. We pass a bird-filled plaza and come to the café, a little room in the midst of shaded alleys. An old woman points us to a seat. She is talking to an elderly man whose little dog runs around the table where he sits. She laughs and comes over, asks us a question that we cannot understand. We smile, say breakfast in Spanish and Italian, apologize for our ignorance of her mother tongue. The old woman gives a knowing look, and heads to the counter with its displays of pastries and the handwritten menu filled with words vaguely familiar.

Outside, a young couple walks down the slanting alley, seemingly dragged along by an energetic little pup. It barks a greeting to the little dog now resting at the legs of its aged owner. The old woman yells out a greeting, a joke perhaps, and comes to our table with two espressos in tiny ceramic cups. We thank her and she goes back to the counter, chatting with the elderly man who has seemingly pulled a newspaper out of nowhere. Another elderly man comes into the café and greets the occupants, giving us a cursory glance. He takes a seat in the back, where a television quietly displays the morning news. We are too far away to read the headlines.

We are sipping our espressos when the old lady returns balancing two ceramic plates on time-worn hands. On these plates sit steaming croissants: warm ham and melting white cheese snuggled in between. Before we begin to eat, she returns with two glasses of orange juice, cool and sweet.

It is perhaps the best meal we have had in months, a simple wordless understanding between two young foreigners and a woman who (in my wandering imagination) has never been away from the reassuring Iberian sun. For a precious few minutes, we are no longer foreigners in

Portugal. We are sons, neighbors, friends; old acquaintances stopping by on our way to the saline-scented shore.

The old woman and the elderly man are laughing. Her laugh is shrill but reassuring, his deep with a hint of melancholy. We devour the croissants but sip the juice, not wanting to leave the little café and its aged inhabitants. The sun climbs over the nearby buildings, slight streams of light trace the windows and tiled floor.

Leaving the café, we place dirty Euros on the counter and thank her in whatever language that chooses to pass through our lips. She smiles, and pulls out a little English, "Thank you." We emerge from the nameless café into the alley, a warm ocean breeze finding its way through the maze of alleyways like a hapless tourist...

FOODS THAT CAN HELP BOOST YOUR MOOD

Dark chocolate contains neurotransmitters that release endorphins in the brain, which can trigger a feeling of pleasure. Consuming dark chocolate in moderation has been shown to lower stress hormones in your body. Opt for 70% dark chocolate to ensure maximum benefits.

Salmon and other fatty fish are high in omega-3s, which can help fight depression and mood swings, as well as improve your memory and focus.

Green tea is full of theanine, an antioxidant which acts as a calming agent.

Almonds are high in a compound called tyrosine, which is one of the building blocks for the production of dopamine and other mood-associated neurotransmitters.

FOOD TIP: When sauteing onions, add a pinch of baking soda to speed up browning and cut your cooking time in half.

Asparagus is one of the top plant-based sources of tryptophan, which serves as a basis for the creation of serotonin, one of the brain's primary mood-regulating neurotransmitters.

Spinach and other leafy greens, such as **kale**, are high in folate, a natural B-vitamin that helps the brain create serotonin. There have been numerous studies linking low folate and serotonin levels to depression.

In addition to tryptophan, **turkey** has high amounts of phenylalanine, an essential amino acid the brain uses to create dopamine, a neurotransmitter that activates several of the mind's pleasure centers.

Avocados contain vitamin B3, a serotonin-boosting ingredient. They also contain omega-3s which have been linked to brain health and mood regulation.

Greek yogurt is packed with large amounts of calcium (more than you'll find in milk or regular yogurt), which causes the brain to release happiness-inducing neurotransmitters.

Honey contains kaempferol and quercetin, which helps to prevent depression by reducing inflammation in the brain.

Coconuts contain medium-chain triglycerides, special fats that fuel better moods and promote general brain health.

TRY THIS!

Create a snack box filled with some of your favorite non-perishable foods in an area where you spend a lot of your time (like your work space or bedroom). This will allow you to grab a quick bite when you're feeling snacky or need an energy boost.

EAT TO LIVE

BY SIOBHAN GORDON

THE COVENANT OF THE WING
By Samantha Allen

PHOTO BY MICHAEL SAECHANG

Sisters of the wing, hear my words.

The buffalo wing cannot be consumed idly. Unlike its lesser sibling, the buffalo chicken tender, the buffalo wing demands attention. Each wing is its own encounter, a happy meeting of lips and sauce, a sensual dance of teeth and bone. The buffalo wing's tasty treasures are not offered freely; they must be accessed, unlocked, savored.

The buffalo wing is crispy. The sauce should mute the crunch without drowning it. The song of the wing is but a few measures long; it lasts but a few bites before coming to a close. Those few bites must have a perfect texture. Flavor, heat, dressing: all these are meaningless in the absence of a crisp exterior.

The buffalo wing is hot. The sauce has bite while still allowing the flavor of the cayenne to shine through. Tongue-scorching, nine-alarm fire wings are for acolytes who do not fully understand that the secret of the wing lies in its balance, a delicate line between heat and flavor, texture and tenderness. To reduce the wing to its Scoville rating, to regard it as a plaything in some childish game of chicken is to disrespect the art of the wing.

The buffalo wing is accompanied by bleu cheese dressing. Not ranch dressing. Under no circumstance, should the buffalo wing be served or consumed with ranch dressing. Ranch dressing is for garden salads and club sandwiches and grandma's fridge. Bleu cheese is for buffalo wings and buffalo wings are for blue cheese. This spicy symbiosis is a bond that cannot be broken.

The bleu cheese dressing must contain chunks of bleu cheese. If the bleu cheese is macerated into oblivion, the dressing becomes nothing but a dull, flavorless paste. There are those who would deny bleu cheese, who would wrinkle their noses at the thought of its color, its taste, its smell. They may still eat buffalo wings, yes, but they are not permitted to enter into the covenant of the wing.

The buffalo wing is a high-contrast food. The color of the wing should be a vibrant orange on a white porcelain plate. The bleu cheese dressing must be cold, not lukewarm, so that the wing's temperature is offset by a slight chill on the lips. In this sense, the buffalo wing is, perhaps counter-intuitively, much like a hot fudge sundae.

The buffalo wing is not just for bars or football fans; it is fine dining whether you make wings at home or pick them up around the corner. The buffalo wing is not an appetizer; a plate of wings can be a full meal. And the buffalo wing is not just a food; it is a lifestyle.

This is our covenant of the wing. So let it be.

TRY THIS!

Freeze yogurt in an ice cube tray and use instead of ice to get a thicker, richer smoothie.

HOW TO: PIT AN AVOCADO

By Adrienne Fox

1. With a medium-sized knife, cut the avocado in half lengthwise around the seed by holding on half securely or placing on a cutting board.
2. Grasp one half of the avocado in each hand and twist one side. One half of the avocado should come away from the seed.
3. This next step is not for the faint of heart. Fold a kitchen towel into quarters. Place the towel and the half of avocado with exposed seed in your hand. Then, carefully, take the knife and tap the exposed seed with the sharp edge of the knife to lodge the knife in the seed. Using the knife handle, gently twist the seed (parallel to

the face of the avocado). The seed should pop out of the avocado and be on the knife blade.
4. To remove the seed from the knife, tap the seed (near the knife blade) against the interior edge of a mixing bowl while keeping the blade above the rim of the bowl. This should provide enough resistance to dislodge the seed from the knife. You want to knock the pit off the blade without damaging you or the blade!
5. Next, slice or dice the avocado with a paring knife and use a spoon to scoop it from the skin. Or use that spoon to eat the avocado out of the skin with a little sea salt!

CHOCOLATE AVOCADO PUDDING

This is a wonderful chocolate pudding dessert that can be made to accommodate gluten/grain/sugar/dairy intolerances without any compromise to taste!

Ingredients:
1 large or 2 small ripe avocados, peeled
1/4 cup cocoa powder, sifted
1/4 cup honey or raw agave nectar
1/4 cup cream, whole milk, coconut milk or almond milk (you can substitute with your choice of milk)
1 teaspoon vanilla extract
1 ounce chocolate of your choice roughly broken into pieces (roughly half a bar of chocolate, optional)

The measurements are just approximations and can be adjusted according to your personal preferences. Some people like it more or less sweet, some people like less cocoa powder. You can experiment with this small batch recipe to get the exact perfect delicious flavor you love!

Directions:
1. Put all the ingredients except for the chocolate in a food processor and blend until smooth. Taste and adjust ingredients as needed.
2. (Optional) Add roughly broken piece of chocolate and blend again.

This gives the pudding some texture with small chunks of chocolate.
3. Top with fresh fruit or whipped cream. Chill in the refrigerator before serving.

SUMMER SANGRIA
By Kristine Hassell

Gulf Coast summers are brutal and unforgivably humid. I have fond memories of summer nights with friends, enjoying backyard BBQs and open house parties that went until dawn. Cold beer and pitchers of sangria were commonplace alongside the bowls of homemade guacamole and that beloved crockpot cauldron of bubbling chile con queso.

As my friend circle aged, our gatherings became a little more structured and the menus changed a little. Now don't get me wrong, you will still find bowls of homemade guacamole and that crock pot of queso bubbling like Old Faithful but you'll also find crudités and hummus to balance out that plate. What hasn't changed is my love of sangria, that fruity concoction that can be a stunning centrepiece to your summer fun.

Maybe there's not a lot of money in the discretionary fund. Send out some invites to your best friends and pool your collective resources for a summer sangria day! Head to the Farmers Market, buy some fresh fruit, and have fun. It is a great way to spend time with friends, relaxing with a night of self-care while you enjoy the (sauced) fruits of your labour!

First, grab a couple of bottles of inexpensive red wine. I cannot stress this enough. Fancy wines will be lost in the melange of fruit that's about to kick off so snag some Two-Buck Chuck and let's do this!

Start with a pitcher and a mixing spoon. Take seasonal fruit like grapes, melon, peaches, apricots, whatever is in season. I love including slices of orange, lemon, and lime, tossed in with the seasonal fruit. Peel and slice your selected fruit until you get about 2 cups. I usually have frozen unsweetened berries around so I'll use those as ice cube garnish in the individual glasses. If you can get fresh strawberries, maybe use frozen blueberries as the garnish, and so on.

Throw that fruit in your pitcher and add your wine. Here's where you get to experiment again! I usually use 1/2 c (or more) of Cointreau or Triple Sec but you can use brandies or light rum instead. Add between 1/4 to 1/2 cup of juice, you can use orange or pomegranate, think about what flavours you've used already and choose something that complements. Give it some extra flavour with about 1/2 c of mixer like seltzer or club soda, again this is your choice. And that's it. It's that easy.

If you're doubling up this recipe, maybe a punch bowl might be better suited for your mixing. Then folks can just ladle their sangria into their wine goblets as they see it. Have spoons or straws on hand for guests to fish out those besotted morsels of fruit.

Another pro tip: mix your wine, Cointreau (or Triple Sec), and fruit into a pitcher. Cover and let marinate for about an hour in the fridge. The longer it rests, the more intense the flavour! When you're ready to serve, stir several times to redistribute the fruit. Here's where you'd add that club soda or seltzer mixer, if you've gone that route.

Enjoy!

TRY THIS!

Assemble all your ingredients in one place before you cook to avoid stressing out over lost ingredients in the middle of the cooking process. Also, arrange the utensils and other tools you're going to need for a more organized cooking experience.

34

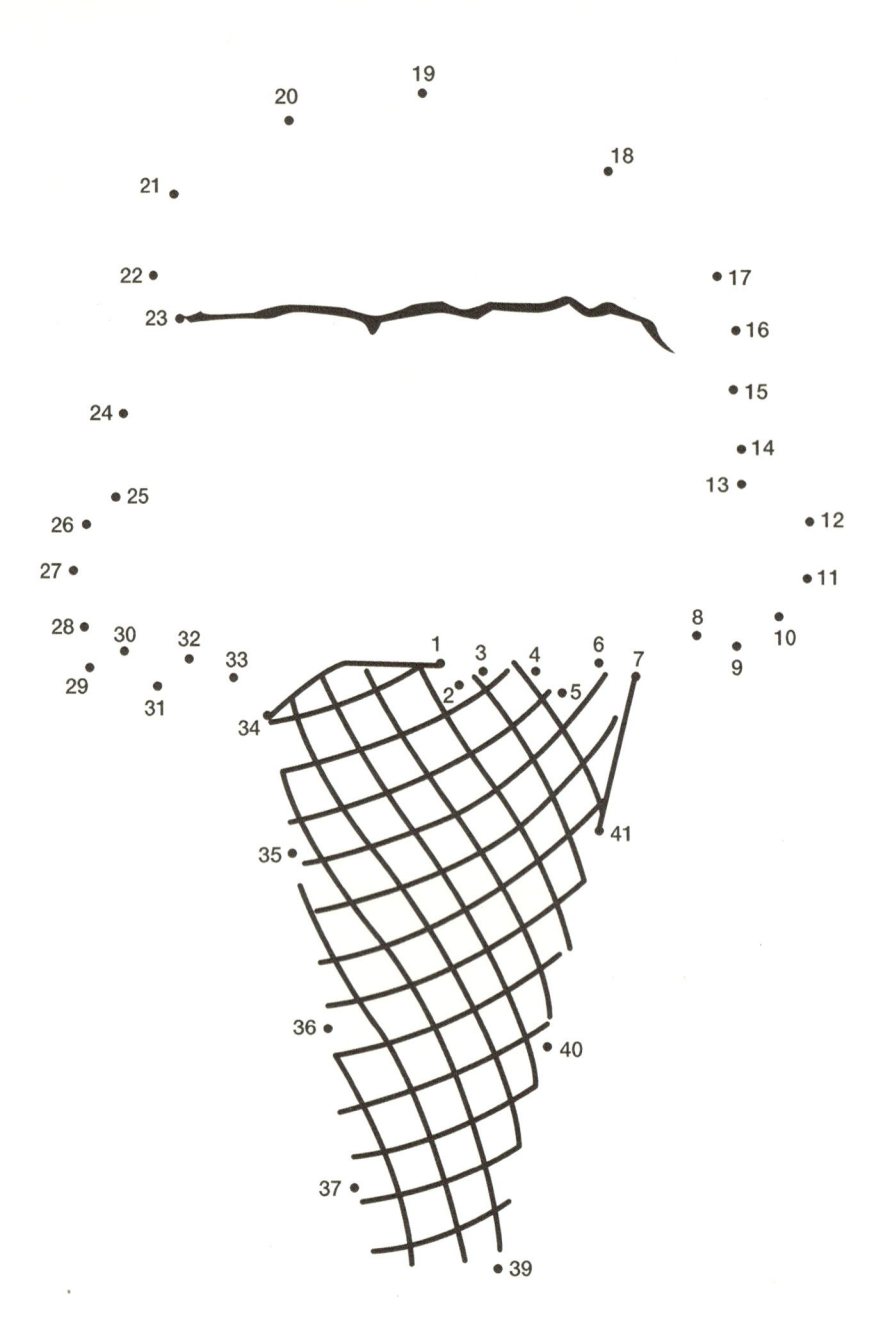

EATING WHILE ON YOUR PERIOD

Beans, leafy greens, and a lean piece of meat (extra-lean beef and skinless white-meat poultry) are great sources of iron that will help restore your body's balance.

Salmon and tuna are loaded with omega 3's and other fatty acids that are great for relaxing the muscles in your body, decreasing the severity of your cramps. Walnuts, flax seeds, and chia seeds also contain omega-3's if fish ain't your thing.

Citrus fruits are a natural diuretic which can help alleviate bloating. Foods rich in magnesium (beans, tofu, peanuts, etc) are also thought to reduce bloating.

One of the very best ways to help decrease water retention, even though it may seem counterintuitive, is to increase water consumption.

When progesterone peaks, the bowel slows down. High-fiber dishes like brown rice, barley, and vegetables will combat constipation while keeping your energy up.

Eating bananas can help regulate your bowel movements.

Whole grains are rich sources of fiber and vitamin B-6, which can help keep menstruation-related hunger at bay, as well as alleviate PMS.

Green vegetables are high in calcium, magnesium and potassium, which help relieve and prevent the spasms that lead to cramping pain. Dark green vegetables also contain high amounts of vitamin K, which is needed to coagulate blood and prevent excess bleeding.

Ginger tea may be helpful in relieving nausea and bloating, and chamomile tea also contains properties that relieve muscle spasms and reduce the tension that can lead to anxiety and irritability.

FOOD TIP: Grate organic lemon rinds and freeze. Add lemon zest to salads, smoothies, cold and hot tea, and water.

VEGAN COOKIE RECIPES
By Kate Lowe

PILLSBURY-LIKE VEGAN SUGAR COOKIES
Ingredients:
2 cups flour
3/4 cup sugar
2 tsps vanilla extract
1 tsp baking powder
1 egg replacer (Ener-G, or apple sauce)
1 stick vegan butter
2 tbsp oil
1/4 tsp salt

Directions:
1. Pre-heat oven to 350 degrees.
2. Cream together egg replacer, sugar, buter, vanilla, and oil.
3. Add dry ingredients to sugar mix and stir.
4. Bake for 10-15 minutes.

PUMPKIN OATMEAL COOKIES
Ingredients:
2 cups flour
1 1/3 cup rolled oats
1 tsp baking soda
3/4 salt
1 tsp cinnamon
1 tsp nutmeg
1 2/3 cup sugar
2/3 cup canola oil
2 tbsp molasses
1 cup canned pumpkin puree
1 tsp vanilla extract

Directions:
1. Pre-heat oven to 350 degrees.

2. Oil large baking sheet.
3. Mix together flour, oats, baking soda, salt and spices.
4. In a separate bowl, mix together sugar, oil, molasses, pumpkin, and vanilla.
5. Combine contents of both bowls together.
6. Fold in raisins and pecans (optional).
7. Drop large spoonfuls onto baking sheets.
8. Bake for 16 minutes at 350 degrees.
9. Remove from oven and put your cookies onto a wire rack to cool.

CHOCOLATE CHIP OATMEAL NUT COOKIES
Ingredients:
1/3 cup peanut butter
2 tbsp canola oil
1 cup sugar or sucanat
1/3 cup soy or almond milk
1 tsp vanilla extract
1 cup flour
1/2 tsp baking soda
1/2 tsp salt
1 cup rolled oats
1/2 cup milk-free chocolate chips

Directions:
1. Pre-heat oven to 450 degrees.
2. Oil large baking sheet.
3. Whisk together the first 5 ingredients and stir to combine.
4. Drop large spoonfuls onto baking sheet and bake for 8 minutes.

TRY THIS!

When baking cookies, chill your dough before putting it on your baking sheet. This allows the leavening ingredients to work before the butter melts out and your cookies lose their texture.

ONE POT SPAGHETTI ALLA PUTTANESCA WITH CHICKPEAS & ARTICHOKE

By Sarah from Yup, It's Vegan - www.yupitsvegan.com
Recipe reprinted with permission.

PHOTO COURTESY OF YUP, IT'S VEGAN

Ingredients:

12 oz. whole wheat spaghetti (you should not substitute for this; see notes)
2 oz. sliced black olives (up to 4 oz. for olive lovers)
1 (14-oz.) can artichoke hearts, rinsed, drained, and chopped
3/4 cup cooked chickpeas
2 tbsp capers
1/2 large white or yellow onion, minced
2 cloves garlic, minced
1 (14-oz.) can diced tomatoes, low sodium or no salt added
1 tbsp dried oregano
1 tsp dried basil
1/2 tsp dried thyme
1/2 tsp red pepper flakes (reduce to 1/4 tsp if sensitive to heat)

FOOD TIP: After working with garlic, rub your hands vigorously on your stainless steel sink for 30 seconds before washing them to remove the odor.

1/2 tsp ground black pepper (reduce to 1/4 tsp if freshly ground)
Salt (see notes)
3 cups vegetable broth, low sodium or no salt added

Directions:
1. Add the pasta to a large, deep skillet, breaking in half if needed (a saucepan may also work).
2. Add the rest of the ingredients, minus the broth, to the pan on top of the pasta (artsy arrangement not necessary!)
3. Pour the vegetable broth over everything.
4. Cover the pan and bring to a boil. Reduce to a steady simmer (medium to medium-low heat) and, keeping covered & stirring occasionally, cook for 8-10 more minutes, or until pasta is done through.

Notes:
The starch from the whole wheat pasta thickens the broth into a mild sauce and that's what makes this recipe work its magic. Gluten-free pasta will almost definitely not be a viable substitute, as it does not have the same properties. Regular (not whole wheat) pasta is what the original recipe used, and it called for more liquid (4 cups). I personally have not tested with anything other than whole wheat.

My olives, artichoke hearts, chickpeas, capers, and tomatoes all came from (BPA-free) cans, so I found that I didn't need to add any salt, even with my homemade salt-free vegetable broth. It's easiest to salt to taste after the pasta is done cooking, but if none of your ingredients have salt added, I recommend adding a bit before cooking in order to get the same results that I did.

In my picture the onions are chopped, but they will do a better job cooking through if you mince them. Sorry for the visual deception.

Finally, I have heard some feedback that the leftovers can get soggy. I think you can minimize the chances of this by: 1) cooking the pasta to al dente, 2) tossing with a bit of olive oil before you store it, and/or 3) let it fully cool, uncovered, before storing.

sometimes... I just really need to bake.

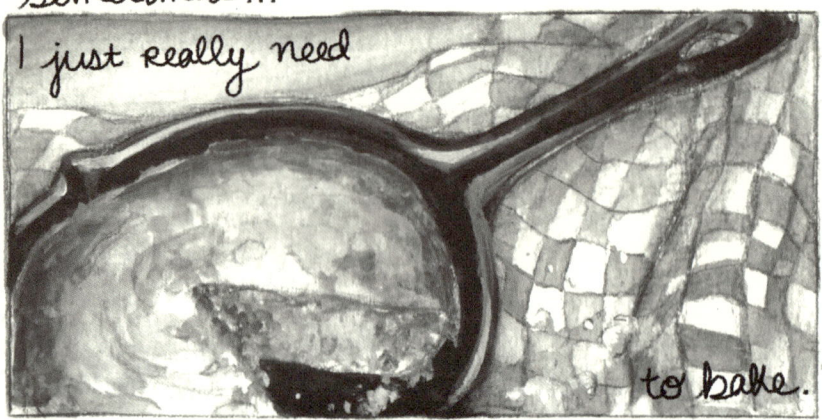

sometimes its to indulge a craving for something sweet like molasses, rich like chocolate or tart like lemon.

sometimes its to share because for me, the giving of food is a way of saying "I care about you, your body, your health."

BY LAUREN JORDAN

and sometimes... its just because I love it.

I love quality ingredients

so delicious on their own

that I can't wait to taste them combined.

I love the physicality of mixing by hand

as an exercise in stress-relief

and the occasional taste-test just to be sure everything is coming out right.

and I love the wait - those moments after the work and before the reward.

during this time I allow myself to exist just in that moment,

to be calm,

while I breathe in the scent of baking.

HOMEMADE DINNER ROLLS

By Jade Gordon

I wanted a sweeter, eggier version of a dinner roll. This turned out the most like any light, fluffy, mass produced dinner rolls I've ever made. They're kinda sublime fresh from the oven with butter. This makes about 35 rolls.

Ingredients:

1 cup sweet rice flour
3 cups unbleached white flour
1/2 cup white whole wheat flour
2 heaping tablespoons oatmeal
1 tsp if you use it as a topping, 1/4 cup roasted flax seed if you want to mix it in
1 packet of yeast
3 tbsp honey
2 tbsp maple syrup
4 tbsp butter
2 eggs
1/4 cup milk
2 tbsp sea salt

Directions:

I used a bread machine, so, everything in, "dough" setting. After the machine's mixing and rising cycles, I formed the rolls, put them close together on a silpat lined baking sheet (parchment would be a good option instead, but foil or foiled paper might burn the bottoms a little), and let them rise until they were at least doubled in size. Bake from room temperature, oven set at 400F for about 17 minutes.

TRY THIS!

Forgot to take the butter out? Soften it quickly by cutting a stick into pieces and placing on a plate, then cover with a metal bowl that's been rinsed with hot water.

Best Popcorn!!

What you need: olive oil + pot + popcorn kernels + bowl

① pour just enough oil in the pot to cover the bottom. pour just enough kernels in the pot to cover the bottom

② offset lid on top of pot

③ put on stove at med-high

④ wait for popping to begin

⑤ once the corn starts to pop, agitate the pot intermittently to move the popped corn up and the kernels down

⑥ as the pot fills, shake the popped corn out into the bowl using the lid as a shield then place pot back on stove and repeat until most of the kernels are popped

⑦ put any of the following on top: salt, butter, parmesan, ranch powder, gruyere, cinnamon, sugar, curry, rosemary, or whatever else you want!

⑧ put it in your face.

by Deanna Poppe

BY DEANNA POPPE

Stress BAKing By Stevie Wilson!

Stevie's Grammie's Peanut Butter Cookies

Things you'll need:

1 1/2 c - Flour
1/2 t - Soda
1/2 c - Butter
1/2 c - Sugar
1/2 c - Brown sugar
1 - Egg slightly beaten
1/2 c - Peanut butter
1 t - Vanilla
1 Bag of peanut butter chips

*If you have a cute apron thats a plus

2

So **what** if you're a nervous wreak?

Cream that butter and sugar together!

3

Find new life purpose as you:

Mix your dry ingredients

Flour   Baking soda

4

Melt that peanut butter!

It's your call if you use chunky or half chunky/ half smooth.

5

Wow OK, exciting. Maybe by this point you aren't shaking from anxiety!

Add the peanut butter to the sugar mixture. And the egg

FOOD TIP: Dry wet food thoroughly before frying to prevent oil from splattering.

⑥ Wow I almost feel like not a fuck up.

Slowly add in dry ingredients

Plus peanut butter chips

⑦ Mix well, reflect some more on your life.

⑧ Add vanilla

⑨ Make sure you pre-heat the oven to 350.

⑩ Put parchment down on the tray

to keep the cookies from burning like your life!

⑪ Spoon out the dough in small balls

FOOD TIP: Reheating pizza slices in a frying pan on low for 2-3 minutes will keep your crust crispy and toppings hot and moist.

Use a fork to gently press down and give the cookies hatch marks.

Bake for 10-12 minutes until golden on top and no longer wet looking

I'm going to stress eat the **hell** out of these!

Congratulations you have channeled your anxious energy into edible comfort! Huzzah!

FOOD STAPLES FOR COOKS ON A BUDGET

By Jon Conley

OVERNIGHT OATS: It practically makes itself. Try soaking rolled oats in milk or yogurt, overnight, add a little bit of sugar, or peanut butter (whatever sounds good to you – there are no rules); maybe throw in some nuts and berries before you sit down to eat it.

MARINATED MEAT: Marinating or using a brine (soaking overnight in a liquid with salt); add more flavor and moisture to tough or cheaper cuts of meat; typically, the longer something soaks, the better it tastes (best results are overnight). I always recommend that people on a budget buy chicken legs or thighs. A package of legs will run you about $3, and they can be seared or stewed to make some of the best dishes.

LENTILS / BEANS: Cheap, filling and quick; easily transformed into soups and curries, with little-to-no effort.

BULK RICE: Go to a wholesale club and buy a 25lb bag of Jasmine rice. That bag will last you half a year, and will cost you ~$17. Cook it in a pot (or a rice cooker if you own one) and serve with chicken and/or steamed or stir-fried vegetables for a filling (and quick) meal.

FROZEN VEGETABLES: Grab a bag of mixed frozen vegetables (bulk shopping is cheaper). It's cheap and it's easy nutrition. All you have to do is boil salted water, or microwave the veggies. Mix with rice and a dab of your favorite sauce, and you have a basic meal. Add a scrambled egg for extra protein and fat.

FRESH FRUIT: Bananas, apples, oranges, berries – whatever is in season will be the cheapest. Trader Joe's is typically the cheapest for a lot of it. All of it has benefits, and all of it can be added to just about any meal. Ever made a spinach salad with apples and berries? You definitely should.

DRIED FRUIT & NUTS: Great for snacking throughout the day; keep some in your bag; Trader Joe's non-sulphured, no-sugar-added mango is great; raw cashews and walnuts are also quite delicious and healthy alternatives to junk food. Check the bulk food aisle at your grocery store. Grab some Craisins (great in salads).

EGGS: Cheap, quick, and high in fats and protein. The egg is the mark by which all cooks and chefs are judged. Everything starts with an egg. Start with simple scrambled eggs.

YOGURT: A great replacement for milk, with the added benefits of cultured enzymes which help with digestion. I like to make fruit parfait with granola and berries with my yogurt.

GRANOLA: A great and versatile cereal alternative which can be enjoyed in a bowl with dairy, or out of a baggie, as a quick snack. You should always have some granola handy.

FOOD CONTAINERS FOR LEFTOVERS: If you're going to cook, it's smart to keep a portion or two for leftovers. It's a great motivator when you're feeling depressed, and a delicious meal is waiting for you in the fridge.

Tip: *If you're in a really bad spot, check to see if you qualify for EBT Basic Food (subsidized government food stamps), visit local food banks or volunteer programs, and buy in bulk (from wholesale clubs).*

Comfort Foods

You look lovely today

We are so proud of you

Your feelings are valid

I love you

BY JEN FOWLER

CHUNKY TOMATO SOUP

By Kathleen Merryman

Ingredients:
1 stick of butter or margarine
1 large or two small onions, coarsely chopped
2 cloves garlic, finely chopped or pressed
6 large tomatoes, chopped
About 1/2 cup flour
2 quarts of milk
1 teaspoon celery salt (plain salt will do)
1/2 teaspoon pepper (paprika or crushed, dried red peppers add extra kick)
3 tbsp sugar
1 tbsp each chopped parsley, basil and tarragon

Directions:
1. Melt the butter in a large soup pot.
2. Add onions and garlic and cook until they are translucent.
3. Toss in the tomatoes and stir often until they soften.
4. Work quickly here: Add the flour all at once and stir it in rapidly to make a vegetable roux. Gradually stir in the milk and stir until all of it is added.
5. Add the sugar, salt, pepper and herbs. Simmer on low to medium heat, until it is hot enough to serve with buttered toast.

"For someone who has not been in the kitchen, [cooking] is a physical statement of self-care - it's literally standing up for yourself and your own food."

Annie B. Kay, Kripalu Lead Nutritionist

REACHING FOR NEW RECIPES

By Adrienne Fox

I love a good burger. When I am feeling low or stressed, I go for a Tavern Double at Red Robin or a mushroom-Swiss at nearly any other joint. Since I have become more aware of my good and bad habits in self-care, more and more I reach for a new cookbook, recipe, ingredient, or technique in my own kitchen instead of running off for a burger. I don't always feel great stress-eating burgers, but I do feel good about myself after trying out a new recipe or cookbook.

For me, cooking accomplishes the things I need to reset and relax: taking time to read and plan, shopping, learning, experimenting, and creating—all aspects of me that I lose to a busy life yet need to maintain to feel grounded and centered. Sometimes I choose simple recipes and other times more complex. Some dishes turn out awesome and some not-quite-as-good (but the learning process is the same). Some culinary explorations take a significant time and money investment, while other dishes are done fast or on the cheap.

Trust me! Cooking for yourself (and others) is gratifying. Even you are new to cooking or afraid of your kitchen appliances, you can do this. Just start simple.

My recommendations for home-chef self-care program are:

- Pick up anything by Mark Bittman—he is easy to follow, great with the basics. If some imperial regime took power that ordered all cookbooks burned, I would join the resistance to save my copy of *How to Cook Everything*—it is indispensable.
- Try a cookbook dedicated to your favorite fandom! You can make Wookie Cookies, or Arya's Lemon Cakes, Harry Potter Cauldron Cakes, or Klingon Blood Pie. A Google search will turn up more novelty cookbooks than you ever imagined. (Beware that some of the recipes in the novelty cookbooks lack crucial details or are poorly edited, choose wisely.)
- Madhur Jaffrey is my go-to for the basics of Indian dishes.

- Desserts (and chocolate) are best with Alice Medrich, in my opinion.

I tend to buy cookbooks. But you <u>definitely</u> do not have to. Save that cash for ingredients. Savvy home chefs can save money by using the interwebs:

- Some chefs post their recipes online, like Paula Wolfert's site with Middle Eastern and Mediterranean recipes (<u>http://paula-wolfert.com/recipes.html</u>).
- Lots of blogosphere have already done the leg-work for you and created blogs catering to a certain cuisine, or dietary needs (try <u>http://glutenfreegoddess.blogspot.com</u> or vegan recipes at theppk.com/blog).
- The Kitchn blog is a great resource from soup to nuts! (<u>http://www.thekitchn.com</u>)
- There are too many free recipe sites to mention. Tour a few and find one that has thoughtful reviews and recipes that excite you.
- Ask family and friends for their favorite recipes. You might find Aunt Betty made a killer chili back in the day.

Happy cooking!

FOOD RESOURCES

NO MORE RAMEN
http://no-more-ramen.tumblr.com
A tumblr loaded with easy, budget-friendly recipes for folks with little time and even less money.

BUDGET BYTES
http://www.budgetbytes.com
This website has tons of easy recipes for those planning meals on a budget.

THE SPOON THEORY
http://www.butyoudontlooksick.com/wpress/articles/written-by-christine/the-spoon-theory/
Christine Miserandino's personal story and analogy of what it is like to live with sickness or disability.

LOW SPOONS FOOD
http://lowspoonsfood.tumblr.com
A tumblr for spoonies filled with recipes and tips that take the lowest amount of energy as possible.

SUPERCOOK
http://www.supercook.com
A free service that helps you determine what meals you can cook with the ingredients you already have on hand.

MEASUREMENT CONVERTER
http://www.food.com/library/calc.zsp
A handy dandy measurement converter for your cooking needs!

DEPRESSION-ERA GRANDMA IN TRAINING
http://depressioneragrandmaintraining.blogspot.com
A blog featuring "Food your grandma would recognize on a budget your grandma would approve."

FEEDING AMERICA FOOD BANK LOCATOR
http://feedingamerica.org/foodbank-results.aspx
Feeding America is the nation's leading domestic hunger-relief charity. Their food bank network includes 200 food banks across the country.

SUPPLEMENTAL NUTRITION ASSISTANCE PROGRAM (SNAP)
http://www.fns.usda.gov/snap/apply
SNAP offers nutrition assistance to millions of eligible, low-income individuals and families. Learn more about the program and apply online to receive benefits.

SNAP RETAILER LOCATOR
http://www.fns.usda.gov/snap/retailerlocator
A website where you can find retailers that serve SNAP EBT customers in your area.

SNAP-ED CONNECTION RECIPE FINDER
http://recipefinder.nal.usda.gov
Search recipes by various categories – including cost per serving or per recipe. You can create your own personalized cookbook by adding recipes you've selected.

ZINE CONTRIBUTORS

Rachelle Abellar
Samantha Allen
Jon Conley
Jen Fowler
Adrienne Fox
Jade Gordon
Siobhan Gordon
Kathleen Gros
Kristine Hassell
Sarah E. Hoffman
Adam Johnson
Lauren Jordan

Kate Lowe
Danielle Martin
Erica McGillivray
Kathleen Merryman
Dale O'Flaherty
Deanna Poppe
Sean Poppe
Anita Sarkeesian
Antonia Tsangaris
Stevie Wilson
Yup, It's Vegan